Jehanne Mehta is a singer, songwriter, and poet who has been writing poems since childhood and songs since her twenties. Her first book of poems, *The Burning Word*, was published in 1991. Since then she has published four further collections of poems and recorded six albums of songs. A definitive collection of her songs, *Earth Songs*, was published in 2024. Her writing, emerging from her own inner journey, is committed to transformation and is a plea to awaken to our inner selves and to the Earth. She has three grown-up children and lives in Gloucestershire with her husband and musical partner, Rob.

Also by Jehanne Mehta:

Poetry
The Burning Word
A Way to Meet
The Difficult Gate
Walking Two Ways
Heart of Yew

Songs
Song Hunt
Earth Songs

Albums
Jehanne Mehta
Green Jack
Pathway with a Heart
Rose in Deep Water
Emblem
This Place

Jehanne Mehta

ENTERING THE NARROWS

SELECTED POEMS

AWEN
Stroud

Published by Awen Publications 2025
12 Belle Vue Close, Stroud, England
www.awenpublications.co.uk

Cover design: Kirsty Hartsiotis
Editing and typesetting: Anthony Nanson
Proofreading: Richard Selby

ISBN 978-1-906900-62-5

For more information about Jehanne Mehta visit:
https://www.jehannemehta.com

I dedicate this book to Jay Ramsay and Bob Harper in thanks for their recognition, encouragement and support of my writing over many years.

Contents

6 LOVE

7 PANDEMIC

8 MISCELLANEOUS

9 SPIRITUAL

Foreword

Ever since I wrote an introduction to Jehanne Mehta's pamphlet *A Way to Meet*, back in 1999, I often feel as though I am moving within the expansive bounds of her poems whenever I go outdoors. Her ability to observe, clarify and extol the natural world still speaks to me on walks through the lanes and fields of the valleys we both live in. I often find myself 'listen[ing] back along [her] trodden tracks of story', and phrases and images rise again and again in my head.

Not that one needs to live in the same town as her to appreciate Jehanne's writing; the intent stillness of her observation, the way she 'holds each drop of dew / suspended in its own light', is alive with a universal music. Each poem, each 'drop of dew', is rich with ways to move the reader beyond the merely physical.

That Jehanne is also a musician, then, should come as no surprise to anyone finding themselves lost within the pages of this book, even if they have never heard her sing. She writes with an ear intently open to all the musics of the world and our species' place within it, with 'warm sun-filled silence[s] ... overflowing with listening'. As the late Jay Ramsay noted, she is 'a poet whose lyrical roots in the troubadour and folk tradition embrace a penetrating contemporary intensity and sensitivity'.

This selection of her poems, gathered and garlanded from decades of writing, is compelling and conclusive proof of Jay's point. Poems of potent, deeply focused observation sit alongside elegies and poems of ecospiritual intensity and need. Intertwined with these are poems that deal explicitly with political and religious themes.

What binds them all together, what makes this such a cohesive book, is Jehanne's continued, exact and exquisite focus on the natural world, from the 'maiden green leaf spurting from a twig's tip' in Stroud's old cemetery, to the suggestion, in 'The Garden', that someone must have 'planted fennel, rosemary, lavender / in preparation for a burial' near to Jesus' burial place.

Though these poems often move with the intensity of dreams – the kind that draw you inexorably into their most resonant images and symbols – their true power lies in the rootedness of Jehanne's language and how it allows the reader to move without blinking between worlds.

Adam Horovitz

1
Stroud

Another Spring

The light struggles up from under, below, beneath
the racing ragged dark, reaching through the
wind flung rain,
targeting the highest, the above watcher,
golden weathercock, on its tall spike pinnacle,
with a quick dull-bright sheen,
for two seconds only ...
but it's enough, a sky glow,
leaving a radiance in your deep most heart.

You know that these storms, whisking the winter world
in this bowl of duns and greys,
where the gutters race with the run-off
of our too concrete reality,
you know these storms cannot drown out
the first faint birdcalls
of another spring,
oh so much more than annual,
an invisible tectonic churning,
seismic shift in your own soil ...

a wakening.

The Cemetery, Bisley Road, 21 March 2008

In Stroud Old Cemetery

I am raw with your supple beauty
this morning in May ...
a maiden green leaf spurting from a twig's tip,
wet bushes dripping aquifers of tears.

They, like me, are seeking a new way.

I am raw with the supple beauty of you, Maiden.
This is the dead rising
in flows of flowers and gold coins of lichen.

I am upended by your wildness.
The graves are overflowing with
tall grasses, sowthistle, hawkbit and poppies.

You push me through myself
until I cannot but emerge

on the summit of myself.

20 May 2001, revised 21 December 2020

Nightfall in the Slad Valley

Skim me the cream of this summer lane
under the owl dusk
shadow wake of green dreams crumpling the valley
while the ancient horns
new dipped in silver
toss in my blood

the night is about its business
on soft wings
the lighted windows shut the houses inwards
but the gardens are alert
stirring under smooth lawn sheets
listening for the wild

slowly
celebrant soul seeps from me
a kind of signature
a scent trailing from me, loud
as a fire flair, for those who peer
out through the bark of trees
and spread dim moisture as they gather
at my back
curious and
welcoming

I'll turn suddenly
with the curdy hedgerows thick
at my shoulder …
turn and wait

open …
open at the heartmost

1999

4

Waymaking

Have you observed the meander of paths,
the paths we make,
never taut,
lines that wind over meadows,
sinuous, loose-curving
between timothy, cocksfoot and clover?

They are unerringly right,
first pencil strokes of a master draughtsman,
dividing to skirt a tree, contour a hillock,
reuniting to lead you out, across, away, into,
among hawthorn and hazel.

We tread them yearly, over and over,
walking this valley ground,
joining up the ways.

We listen back along these trodden tracks of story,
moving from doorstep to woollen mill, farm door to shepherd's hut,
upslope and underwood, over grassland and grazing,
from gate to stile and back to the
humming highroads.

Who passed here centuries along?
Who passes, drawing beautiful traces,
this fine unconscious artistry of feet?

Maybe this is how we love the landscape.
Not knowing, just going about things,
from here to there,

we make paths.

13 July 2006

Story Tree

Standing in a sea of milk white hedge parsley
sparked through with flashes of yellow buttercup,
upright still
in a hollow where cows come to rub
and lace capped with pungent may blossom,
this forgotten little thorn tree
once grew on the edge of a manorial estate
now long since demolished,
leaving only its park of giant oaks.

Ancient, with cracked and wizened trunk
covered in warts, excrescences,
knobs and patches of dead bark
and tiny twisted twigs,
where even now new leaves spill out of crevices,
it has become holder of memories
home of stories
telling of suffering earth.

See this horror here:
a silent scream wide mouthed
while shocked eyes look blankly
into an uncomprehending world.
An aged crone holds one bony hand
across her heart, raked out, emptied of love,
while the other guards her womb and genitals
raped and dried out of all seed capacity.

Did this thorn tree choose to reveal our crimes?
Who chose it to be our memory stick,
in this abundant summer meadow,
still alive after generations of the well-to-do

built on and abandoned this landscape.
Is there hope still in the blossom that unfailingly
emerges in the spring?
Story tree
shocking us awake, if we dare to look.

Siccaridge Wood in July

This warm sun filled silence
is overflowing with listening.
You know you are seen,
heard, welcomed.
There is a questioning in the hot summer air,
a velvet curiosity:
What is your intent?
Do you come here to meet us?

This path beside the shaded water,
overhung with copious bunches of ash keys and
pink tinged sycamore seeds,
this path, is thick with it,
with intense interest in
everything you are ... and
you are almost awake in
this imminent otherworld,
this imminent otherworld of beingness that
holds our world in being.

Here ... now ... it is opening, a narrow crack only,
just enough to let out
commas, fritillaries,
messengers of magic,
rapid flashes of brilliant orange
dancing over a field of
fragrant meadowsweet.

Time has gone on holiday,
leaving you floating in a paradise,
where perfumes catch you suddenly
in patches of shadow and

the trees are alert,
crowding in towards you
along the steep valley banks.

Your senses deepen
beyond our common three dimensions.
Touch becomes an affair
 of the soul, like love.
The trickle of cool water
between your toes,
where the stream flows
(only just in the heat)
under the gnarled and fallen oak,
is a secret your feet had almost forgotten.

Beside the ancient yew a splash
of dappled light reveals
a familiar form,
small, neat, horned and hoofed,
cross-legged
at your side,
and your inner ear might catch
a snatch of distant music
from his reed flute.

The warm listening presence
extends into a huge embrace.

You are held in hope,
despite the manufactured
clouds.

16 July 2013

2

Albion

Beltane in England

Oh, this festival of green,
rolling in torrents over the trees,
in the subtlest shades of surprise,
unfurling a boundless fertility:
saplings sprouting in bundles
from a smile wide as the woods,
dimpled with stitchwort and violets.

And we are expecting some
vast desert doom,
where our waste devours the wild
as we go down as into quicksand
with a last rictus of despair.

But She has other plans:
ivy, beech and birch leaves,
shaking out like handkerchieves
from her fat pockets;
leaf casings, rosy as lips,
littering the lanes,
and everywhere, She is agog
for love.

In the old cemetery even the graves
are beds of tufted grass,
inviting unheard of, secret conceptions.

Did you notice the daisies
eyeing you with sun-sharp intensity?

You could not slip out of this game,
even if you wanted to:

the bluebells are longing to explore
your toes,
and the footways are only
a temporary diversion,
surfaces to be reclaimed
by your feet,
in the wink of a green eye.

And the honeybees did not go far,
still weaving their rapid lemniscatory pollen dances,
behind the knotted veils,
waiting for our love-call
back to the hives.

A child in pink tights clambers on to a wall
and jumps.
Who knows where she will land,
wild clematis in her hair,
her core curriculum coiling green
from her schoolbag,
in long tendrils of exuberant vegetation?

And we are expecting some
vast and desert doom,
where our waste devours the wild
and we go down as into quicksand
with a last rictus of agony.

But oh, this festival of green,
riotous, rejoicing.

And are we now too old for love,
our loving days over?

6 May 2010

Albion?

This model now, maquette of a masterpiece,
is bent out of alignment along the vertical axis,
the clay cracked, dry, crumbling.
It no longer serves.

Take a new baseboard,
take netting, pliers and strong wire
and build her anew;
but this time, around the armature, not clay,
this time build her, like Blodeuwedd, out of flowers,
bluebells, crosswort, lady's smock
and the wild white cherry;
and set a bee house for her heart,
alive with summer harmonies.
She would be a passion of pollination.

You would sense her sweetness
long before you saw her,
her eyes awake,
alight with recognition,
and love would flow like honey
out of her palms.

16 May 2010

14

Make your heart into a hive

Make your centre into a hive
where it is always summer,
sun warmth, blood heat,
encouraging the honey hunt
of the bees
foraging for nectar of love
in the calyces
of open human hearts.

Make your centre into a home
for the bees,
proof against the threats
of parasites and pesticides,
of man-made microwaves and
monocultures of the mind,
the monstrous pride that modifies
the sacred structures of the land.

Make your heart into a hive.
Let it be the face you
shine into the world,
a refuge for the black bees
of Albion, for making that golden mead
rich and royal,
spilling out everywhere
the forgotten gifts
hidden in the heart of these
overridden islands.

Let your heart be a hive.

26 December 2014

15

On Minchinhampton Common

I am walking,
walking barefoot on the common,
on this warm green ground,
ground that belongs only
to itself,
to the four wise winds,
to the treasures it conceals under its
ancient crinkled gown, cow trodden,
unfurling it all along the changing seasons
of the sun,
in subtlest colours of gold, violet,
purple and deep blue,
finely stitched and embroidered with bramble, briar and hawthorn
and spangled with the dew.

This is common ground,
never ploughed,
never dug, since
long forgotten folk
built roundhouses,
buried their dead,
threw up bulwarks against
marauders
and watched the stars,
glimpsed through forest boughs
ages since unseen,
dipping and wheeling
in their round dance
horizon to horizon.

Here I walk on Albion's ground,
her secret spirit still awake,

in spite of the fog that fetters feeling
and tangles thinking into knots we do not
even notice,
her secret spirit still awake,
still calling through our feet;
and do we hear, do we hear
the quiet insistent voice of the ground,
the common ground that belongs only
to itself?

25 September 2011

3

Seasons

New Year

You stand under the gateway
of the year,
sensing it is more than time
you celebrate here,
more than a passage from
one space to another.
You stand on a crossing of
dimensions where
the pain opens to a sunrise,
hatred dissolved by light,
and what is unknown yet,
like the fattening bud on the stark branch,
announces a newness in your heart.

Step over this threshold
of never was, but will be.
The mist has veiled everything known and
what emerges under the lifting clouds
is a landscape refashioned
from the inside, where what is earth
and what is your heart
run together now.

Snow

Look:
there are white petals
falling from the sky, as if,
in the fields of heaven,
a wind had stripped
the blossoms of their glory
and here they spin,
frozen into crystal filigree,
down, down and down
into our cold and anxious world.

There are white petals falling,
blanketing the ground in
a strange and luminous silence,
rounding out all the edges,
angles of bitterness
and apathy,
blunting the serried spikes of cynicism
under layer upon layer
of beauty.

Oh look:
there are while petals falling
and our mouths open
in wonder.
For a moment we see differently.
For a moment
we see.

10 January 2010

Look at me

There never was such a one,
such a full cream spring,
frothing and steaming along every bough,
white, fresh, sweet, resounding,
milked by the firm fingers of the sun
from Earth's brimming udder.

You say, maybe, 'Now the sharp shards
of winter wild have fled northwards,
she is all of an urgent scramble
to ascertain a future,
in the face of impending drought.'

But she says, 'Look at me.
Does beauty ever grow from fear?
This fullness lives in you.
Look at my steep shoulder,
home to the bee orchid and the yellow haze
of cowslip keys.
Look and answer me:
where in the convoluted caverns of your
unknown deeps
do my secrets grow?
Could it be that your own joy
lifts the bubbling rapture of the lark?'

19 April 2010

May Moon

May moon, now edging into full …
I could cup it in my hands,
protect it from the rush of cloud shadows
that nightly engulf the heart;
silver mirror, expertly framed by the dance
of stars,
reflecting back to me
this little scrap of attempted humanity;
ball of white crystal in my crook'd fingers,
revealing the countenance of love,
as we, astonished by beauty,
lie in a bed of billowing sighs,
heedless of the drip of hours …
while Pan, taller than ever we imagined,
strides the hills, with the running fox
and the light owl, night winged, gliding,
and buds of beading hawthorn, musk scented
– the delicate opening faces of countless laughing presences –
growing in his hair.

May moon,
caught here in upraised hands,
sister of the night, pearly queen,
midwife of the unborn,
words always shaping, simmering, unspoken,
in the cauldron of my heart.

12 May 2011

A Study

The sill is rotten between out and in. There are
cracks in the joins in the woodwork.
It's hard to come to grips with the weather,
let alone the seasons.
Roses wilt and the damselflies are scarce
but there are strains of music outside, mandolins under the holly tree.
You, however, need to go inside
away from the outburst of summer.
The sill is only a symbol.
You are searching for the fork in the inner road where the choice is
    yours to be
listening for the grace that enlarges,
opening a new vista beyond habit.
Even the clouds here are different.
Have you noticed the road forks here?

16 June 2022

Michaelmas

So quiet up here,
just the westering gold
and the Severn, brilliant,
far away,
gleaming like molten bronze;

only the crows calling,
clatter of pigeon wings;
a few conkers on the grass verge,
shining, irresistible treasure for
my ever hungry pockets, and
white feathers,
always white feathers,
guiding my unknowing feet.

Here is lichen,
daubed haphazard on grey walls,
like gold dust;
scarlet bryony draped over brambles.

My pockets are like my heart,
always gaping wider
for more love gifts ...
from you, or from the Lady,
Lady of all harvests,
unstinting as she is, if only
we know how to open,
how to receive her.

And, above, the glory of
open sky ...
no limits.

This is the fifth dimension
right here, right now.
Everything is alive, awake and
speaking ...
even the grief
even the grief.

If I choose I have only to
retune my ears
and listen,
refocus my eyes
and look.

If I scrape away the dross
the world is

light.

Lypiatt, Michaelmas, 29 September 2009

The Mothering Dark

This is the time of the mothering dark,
the crow black mantle of earth in winter.
She is withdrawing her flame to the centre,
holding it close like a secret treasure.
The meadows are white and the last leaves are tumbling.
Small birds flock together, for forage is scarce.
The way now is down, waking each to a kindling,
kindling of love in the fire of the heart.

4

The Earth

Nothing now common

Heat, honeysuckle, pink poppy heads,
city suited magpies, strutting under limes ...

This morning the pear tree was sounding with bee song,
continual soft intoning, relieving the vortical pull on the spine,
the shattered orientation, unsettling leakage of time.

This is no common spring,
nothing now common,
a reaching through of paradise:

hedges going down under blizzards of blossom,
blackthorn, thornless in its Eden white,
cowslip keys releasing the meadows
and blue, full-blown, fervent,
a blue aflame from beyond itself,
under the leaning beeches.

The unbearable sweetness of flowers
tilts the heart out of its easy axis,
tearing us open, like love.

Beneath our closed faces something unknown turns.
Can we live with this heaving and churning
in the fertile ground,
upsetting certainties, unsettling our roots?

She is taking nothing lying down now.
She is about her rebirth, emerging in the vertical plane ...
She is awake, here ...

inside us.

2010

Hymn to the Earth

She is lovely in the springtime in her dress of gold and purple;
She is lovely in the summer in her robe of living green,
Lovely in the autumn all clothed in flame and yellow,
Lovely in the winter in her gown of mist and rain.

She is lovely where your feet have trod and left a winding pathway,
Lovely where the deer rests in the warmth of evening sun,
Lovely where the buzzard soars on the west wind from the ocean,
Where the trees talk a green language and the restless squirrels run.

She is lovely where the silver brook sings its endless melodies,
Lovely where your hand has shaped the landscape to your will,
Lovely where the ploughman cleaves her depths to plant the harvest,
And when her fields are cold and bare, then she is lovely still.

In rocks and soil she is alive, alert and always listening;
In beech and ash and sycamore she is watching and awake.
You can sense her body tremble as your heart is slowly opening;
You can feel her move towards you as you begin to speak.

All down the twisting centuries she has waited for this moment,
For your heart to sing with her heart and dance to the same beat.
In the woods and hills a new earth stirs beneath her secret portals.
A world which only you and she together can create.

May 2008

Cosmic Shift

Beltane bush fires,
hedge long,
sharp white flames
licking into the blue,
festival fanfare of dandelions
loud in the lanes,
splashing our eyes with gold
after a black winter;
a milky way of daisies
in millions, hiding
who knows how many
undiscovered galaxies
of plant magic,
where mighty beings we do not yet see
weave archetypal forms
up out of the hidden earth.

This sun is more than simple solar radiation ...
the inworking of cosmic shift,
pollination of love,
into our waiting hearts.
This is the mystery the bees teach.
This is why we need the bees.
It is our one opening chance.
Now.

17 May 2013

Incantation

Let there be an oasis of wonder:
white windflowers shaking under the wall ...
starways to heaven;
the great rude, rush of the winds,
loud, strong, strident,
whipping the boughs of the
budding beeches;
the language of blossom
held back until now,
frost closed in April,
and here
singing in clouds of
rose pink, magenta and blush red,
wide lipped for the visiting bees ...
the bees ...
Where are the bees?

Let there be a sanctuary of reverence,
where the folded hands of Earth
reach out in prayer to us,
who have the power, the listening senses,
to re-enchant the world,
creating her anew out of our
inner seeing ...
that alive we could be
to her will, encircling us around.

Let there be an inspiration of harmony,
where the loss we feel when
one single creature ceases to exist
engenders an unstoppable song from the heart
of our humanity,

awakening the will to start again,
drawing hope
out of the abyss.

Oh let us surrender to the opening innocence
that shines through every
unfolding flower.

Let there be an oasis of wonder.

21 April 2013

Markstones

I think you know
we are going beyond paradigms.
We will not let ourselves be held
in boxes or
small, curtained rooms.

We meet at markstones, menhirs
and dolmens
– that *we* once sang into place? –
here, where heraldic beasts,
antlered, horned and hoofed,
where fox and hare, raven and wren,
and the Fair Folk in crowds,
look on with expectation,
here on this sprung and moisty ground,
where bracken and beech leaves redden
and subside, becoming soil and loam;

for here, where we stand, the Old Gods dance
with the future.

Catalytic now, freed out of the private dark,
we are the passionate transition,
the restoration of primordial reverence,
primal innocence,
we are the joining …
we are the joining.

What we are about here, at the markstones,
under the wide wheeling stars,
makes a beeline for the not yet,
calling it to us,
to rebuild the sacred mountains,
the shattered bones,
reignite the spark in the blood,
drawing forth the Deep Light.

No heart will ever be the same after this.

I think you know, don't you?
I think you know:
we are heading out
beyond the paradigms.

We are the joining.

31 December 2010

The Waiting

The waiting is intense;
not a grass blade but knows it,
now time has come off its hinges
and opens all ways.

There is a watching,
a listening, sharp as January shoots
that pierce the patient earth,
a gathering from all four directions:
fur, feathers, and the folk
of the mounds, the stones and of the trees,
the ones we only see with closed eyes,
or imprinted for a moment on bark,
swift caught in water swirls, then gone,
dissolving into
rippling shadows.

Do we dare to be transparent,
fired by the many dimensions of love?
Do we dare to be transparent in this fire,
flame feathered like the phoenix?

For we are the beacon, the burning pillar,
a-shine with eyes,
where what was below is rerouted
to the stars,
what was lost in deep space
reconnects with the heart
of earth.

The waiting is intense;
not a grass blade but feels it,
now time has come off its hinges.

The waiting intensifies.

24 January 2011

Safety in Listening

There has only been one hairy house spider
in the bath this winter and,
though I check every bath time,
for months there have not been any woodlice
in the microfibre cloth I leave between the taps.
They used to like the dampness.
I'd throw them out of the window to start
a new life on the lawn.
I sort of miss them.

The changes are subtle but noticeable:
celandines, snowdrops, daffodils and bluebells
all out at once,
but the tree leaves are slow
still wedded to the old patterns.

Our ancient puss is deaf and nearly blind but
to orientate she uses her sixth sense and smell.
She always knows when we are near.
Like hers my hearing's none too good.
It makes the quality of my listening so important.

I can almost hear what the daffodils
on the kitchen table
are trumpeting so loudly.

Subliminally we know
nothing will be the same now, so
we cling to what we know is safe,
trying to block out the waves
of the unexpected,
desperate,
like the proverbial Englishman,
to be an island again.

Maybe the safety is in the listening,
the soft click of a door not now truly shut
and the wind is rising.

Shall we need, like puss, to orientate with our
sixth sense, release the tried and tested emotions,
be in the unknown instant, alert, and maybe

more free?

15 March 2016

Lullaby of the Earth

Peace my child, child of the white bird, sleep.
Heed not the wail of the storm wind,
Nor the wild of the black wave rising.
Here in the harbour of my breast,
Thy boat shall come to rest.
O child of the white bird, sleep.

Peace my child, child of the red rose, sleep.
Heed not the flames of the furnace,
Nor the seer of the fierce sun burning.
Here in the garden of my breast,
Lay down thy head and rest.
O child of the red rose, sleep.

Peace my child, child of the tall hills, sleep.
Heed not the great rocks rending,
Nor the roar of the world descending.
Here in the valley of my heart
Be still and take thy rest.
O child of the tall hills, sleep.

Peace my child, child of the gold wings, sleep.
Heed not the whirlwind screaming,
Nor the pain of the old days keening.
Here in the temple of my breast,
Oh come in peace to rest.
O child of the gold wings, sleep.

Peace my child, child of the new word, sleep.
Heed not the death of all meaning;
It is only an outward seeming.
Here in the vessel of my heart,

Here love is born again.
O child of the new word, sleep.

Peace my child, child of the white bird, sleep.
Heed not the wail of the storm wind,
Nor the wild of the black wave rising.
Here in the harbour of my breast,
Thy boat has come to rest.
O child of the white bird sleep,
Child of the white bird, sleep.

Song lyric, 1984

5

Know Yourself

Prologue

If you are afraid to fall,
everywhere is edge and
crumbling:

the puddle where the rubble of
the old road rises;

this spring about to uncoil,
all at once in ripples,
out of bole and bough;

the speckled depths in the eyes
of friends,
when words threaten to open the
gulfs of the heart.

Nowhere is safe now;
we could tumble through anywhere,
without warning,
slipping into adjacent landscapes
we have always inhabited,
but with closed eyes,
between breaths.

Everywhere
we are threatened
with awakening.

2012

Sea Riders

Araf
araf
araf nawr
Slow
slow
slow down now.
Stand … stop … before this wide
blue-green expanse of ocean.
Sefwch yma
Wait here, stop
at the edge
until you feel
the rolling rhythm of the tides,
these returning cosmic cycles
that nothing interrupts,
these rolling rhythms that mould us
soul deep.
Foot falling in the sand,
feel the salt lick of the
running wave.
Listen to the
mounting roar and sink
of incoming swell,
the withdrawing rattle of sliding
shingle.
Watch the dipping wing
of kittiwake and guillemot
tumbling among these dark and massy cliffs
where seals sing in hidden
clefts, dolphins dive, and the air stings
sharp against you mouth,
gaping and amazed before this

ocean mystery.
Ignore the man-made clouds that
stripe the sky,
dropping steely rods of rain, deploying drought
like armaments, displacing
the habitual patterns of
wind and weather:
sorcerer's apprentice stuff this,
which we are bound to
drown in
when fear takes over,
feeding on surface insecurity.
But no
Ar agor
Open,
we are open,
open for business
with a deeper magic, allied
to the unstoppable rhythm
of the tides.

We are sea riders,
riders of the deep.

31 July 2013

Feet

Here is the opening,
where your tight valley-bound heart lets go
channels and spreads, tide swung,
on gull-gathering banks, and breathes
breathes wide and far deep as dreaming,
under the whole sky.

Sunrise-gold cockles, like long mislaid hopes,
shine out of the moist receiving sand
and your prayerful feet sink, settle and move on,
cradled safe as you walk
through this sifting, loose lying upwash
of the pounding hammering sea.

Out from Scott's Bay
your explorer's feet dance and run,
over crab scuttling wrinkles and furrows
where you come at a thing sideways,
surpriseways, everything unsought, unthought,
invisible worlds emerging out of the naked,
soft-bellied, teeming, tide-emptying shore.

Southwards along the sea's silver rim,
at a safe distance crouching,
haze blue and ... beautiful,
looms the great Worm's Head;
and this sudden instant
the old worm in your heart unfastens and falls,
leaving only its coiled casts in the sand,
to tread lightfoot in the shallows ...
and the gentle air of this hymned and templed morning
sings soft in your song starved ears.

This is the turning.
You have broken through.

What fear held you, everwhen in the valleys of your days,
gnawing at the secret surfaces of your heart,
if not the terror of being touched
as now you are,
by this warm inflooding tide
of tenderness?

Llansteffan, 1 September 2003

Panning for Gold

It's like panning for gold,
seeking your starborn self,
only the finest few grains glimpsed
among soil and rock dust,
unanticipated crumbs
inside this earthborn, this egoity,
webwork, where the tasks we set
outside time are
tangled and knotted in
soul struggle.

Dare to ask:
who is it says 'I' to yourself?
The one who dimly remembers
the brief you gave yourself, and
the gift of knowing,
before the earthquake of birth,
fragmentation of loss.

Only provisional,
all these centuries,
this we have been, predominantly.
Can you mother this 'I' now,
this gold,
the one who looks out at you
from the mirror,
the beauty that chose
to be you?

28 June 2012

Sonnet I

I'll not rise by the constraints of duty bound,
Or be fettered by fear to the tracks of a linear day,
As clouds hanging over the high morning ground
The sweet shining of the dawn with doubts dismay.
I'll not let the ash of old fires scar my heart,
Nor thought in its tangles trap my waking joy,
Nor let the wings of my unfurling dreams be caught
In the tightening webs which the world will ever try
To convince me are the only and the real.
No: here about my centre gathered warm,
Where I know the truth of the untold love I feel,
I will offer myself on the fragrant bed of time.
    For time itself waits poised upon this move:
    To die through my heart and live again as love.

22 October 1995, dedicated at midsummer 2016 to Jo Cox

Sonnet II

You are so far spread greater than you know:
You track the long trod dismal daily grey,
boned, kerbed and neatly boxed in a clay
border, heart blindfold, not even a toe
out of line, thinking unopened, slow,
no wild verges; yoked to the straitened day.
But at the sluice, dreams, thronging the raceway,
Heave at the wet boards, lunging for the flow.

An angel pounds at your temples, stirs your gut;
the sheer light, landing, grips you like a crown.
He cannot bear these streams diverted, channels cut,
and you to yourself dim wasteland overgrown.
Will you turn the heavy winches of this gate,
before the terrible roar of your own soul breaks it down?

1999

You run, you fall

You run, you fall, you forget, you die
You run, you fall, you forget, you die
You run, you fall, you forget, you die

You are not afraid of dying
but of being beautiful

You are not afraid of oblivion
but of being who you truly are

You are not afraid of falling
but of standing alight on the pinnacle of yourself

You are not afraid of running
but of taking the first single, simple step

Unlock your right shoulder
Unleash your left leg

Who is it pours radiance into the
so long aching earth

but you yourself
in yourself
walking

2004

This is my pain

This is my pain.
I hold it in both hands
like a flower,
because it has grown there,
rooted in my blood and
emerging exactly
when I am ready to see
the beauty,
the fold of petals, nested
each in each, spiralling inward,
when I am ready to know
how to free it upwards
to the sun.

I wait,
unknowing,
for the fruit.

15 November 2009

Wild Edges

We are interwoven with the wild,
always.
The untapped edges of ourselves
creep into the underside
of our consciousness.
Brambles and goosegrass
sticky with unstoppable affection,
tendrils of clematis, bryony and
sweet honeysuckle,
entangle in the unmapped
reaches of our souls, where
the Earth speaks in green whispers
of the Deep Light we have forgotten.

Opening the ears of our hearts
we hear the melodies of flowers
and know the golden palms of the sun behind the sun,
dispensing blessings on our upturned faces.

There is an endless sky beyond the sky,
roots reaching deeper than rocks,
where luminous seeds are awakening,
and a wild laughter, encoiled
around the spindle of our spines.

We are the garden where the Deep Light emerges
laughing,
hand in hand with
the wild edges of the world.

Inspired by Glennie Kindred, 20 July 2015

Octogenarian

How do you manage the shrinking world?
How do you deal with the long fertile roads
your legs cannot reach,
the shapes, the colours,
your eyes can no longer touch,
the words your ears can no longer embrace,
when they are still there
but beyond you now?
You can
walk those remembered ways,
the distant fields of gold,
always still living inside you,
once again, catch those colours like echoes in
your opening mind,
fill the secret jewels hidden in
the words of companions,
clasp
the piping of the blackbird's song
into your beating heart,
that opening doorway at your centre
which one day you will choose
to go through
into a beyond that is perhaps
the blueprint
for here and now.
You may be approaching the Real World.
Who knows how long it will take? Meanwhile,
embrace, wholeheartedly,
that shrinking,
like the warm hug of a close friend.

Can you embrace the shrinking as
a gift?

13 May 2023

Cabin Fever

Look.
Listen.
Your heart pounds in panic,
suspended in the prison of your ribcage,
but your back is resisting the vertical,
curling inwards, knees to chin,
ridged and rigid,
like some ancient ammonite,
protecting the primordial pain.
You are double glazed against the storms of change,
the splitting buds dancing,
the wind ripped sky.
Look.
Listen.
The moment is only now.
Gather your young soul in your arms and carry her out
into the singing green.

12 March 2008

Stone Tool

Somewhere
in the backwoods
of your life,
guarded by the spirits of rock, wind and moss,
you have stored
a stone sarcophagus,
against just such occasions
as this.
Now, battered, floored and aching,
from the sudden encounter with yourself,
you must lie in it
for the requisite three days (however long that may take),
lie in this unconsuming painfire, while angels in overalls
stoke the flames with roses, burning you clean,
burning you clean.

Not knowing when it might come in handy,
somewhere in the backwoods of your life,
guarded by spirits of rock, wind and moss,
under the yew trees
you kept
a stone sarcophagus.

27 February 2008.

Bones and Stones

The hospital scanner revealed
erosion of my fundamental geology,
the substrate of this 'I' land,
I live in, crumbling,
dangerously;

but I am more than
the rock I am built on.
These bones, laid down by the
volcanic activity of love,
fluid, then soft,
hardened to a
framework I could
walk with, work with;

and I now, upright still,
thinking heart, mast to myself,
riding the storm waves,
can hold this structure
into the winds,
roped, muscled,
anchored, sails trimmed,

stronger than stone.

Easter Saturday, 7 April 2012

6

Love

Cathar

Let me not escape from this moment,
Keep me captive in your arms until I see,
From under the wrinkled, earthen lids of time,
The sudden eye of love wink blindingly
And all that ever blossomed, blossom now,
Radiant white, along the blackened bough.

1991

Lemniscate
(the Hanged Man)

You are upending.
Wisdom streams upwards
from below.
You are sole to soul now
with the Earth,
dazzled by her deep Light.

Inversion point.
The crossing at your sun centre
is activated:

total polar reverse ...
shock waves racing, galaxy wide ...

you are hanging into the sky now,

from one foot.

Everywhere,
everywhere,
you see stars
shining,
shining,
shining out
from the hearts of friends.

Love is the shift key.
Love is the shift.

18 November 2008

After the violence

Spreadeagled to the four quarters
stretched out as you are to the farthest edges
it's hard to know that you are crucified

on yourself

and only now it sinks in:
where the long drawn agony tears you apart
in that middle place
just where the knife twists
THERE is love
growing
unstoppable
unwinding the tortured years
with the gentlest touch
reaching upwards to your heart
the way the first snowdrop spears
take their unerring aim for the sun

and every cell of you becomes a heart
beating
beating …
till you are nothing but a myriad of wings
heading into the light

and you are hand-fasted to the future
by a silver cord of blessing
that you will
never cut

January 2009

The Codes of Healing

For Dr Eric Pearl

These are the codes of healing:
when the warmth makes channels
where once was arid,
when your wishes step aside
and there is nothing impeding the subtleties,
the rush of equations,
when you are so naked to the power
of this moment,
you become the irrigation of the parched,
an influx of elements first ever,
alchemical,
you, wearing your wings like lab coats,
silver white.

Now she opens to you,
releasing her gold, from dimensions
undreamed of,
hermetically hidden till now,
homoeopathically pouring out her secrets
into the scripts of your blood,
the recesses of your flesh,
the geometry of your bones.

You have to wake to read them.

These are the codes of healing …
no hesitations …
This is the unheard of
work of love.

1 February 2011

Unicorns

We know about horses:
Sleipnir, Bucephalus, Gringolet,
eight-legged horses, winged horses,
wind racers, silver hoofed;

but we have forgotten what we knew
about unicorns ...
the silence in that garden.

The way we approach one another
matters,
treading softly, not to startle the purity,
distort the spiral flame
between the eyes,
the pressure at the root of the nose.

Is this how the brown earth feels under the
beat of hooves,
how spring air feels the imprint
of lark song?
Is this the way a smile
opens our faces to each other,
heart deep?

We have forgotten what we knew
about unicorns ...
but now,
nothing virtual, nothing digital,
the fabled horn is becoming ... directed lightning,
a radiant flash
of love,

piercing the separation,
a communion,

an instrument of knowing.

3 March 2011

After listening to Rumi I

When I say to you,
'You are lovely,'
you do not believe me,
because of the blemishes
you know so intimately;
but those blemishes are the scars
of your sufferings
and they shine out of your soul,
radiating beauty,
the way the daisies do
in the long summer grasses.
So when I say to you,
'Even with closed eyes,
I still see how beautiful you are,'
it is true.
Believe it.
Believe it.

30 May 2010

After listening to Rumi II

Evergreen Oak
(Recalibration)

Your inner teacher says:
'Come closer.
Be faithful to the tree that you are.
Like last year's leaves,
shed the old stories,
the ache of unfulfilment,
the pain of separation
from yourself.

'Follow the fool's tracks.
He turns himself inside out
and upside down
and all for smiles,
all for laughter,
that splits paradigms
and shakes you to your roots.

'Come inside.
Summer is a wild rose,
though only for a little while,
but your heart is
a rose for all seasons
and wild
for love.

'Do not be afraid to be
heart to heart
with yourself.'

7 June 2010

7

Pandemic

Syrian Dreams

After listening to Maya Youssef

How do you ever say goodbye
to a city with seven gates
each dedicated to a planet
even one to the sun
golden gate to the city of roses
damask roses framing the doorways
to the intimate courtyards of
family life, hung with heavy vines
and bougainvillea?

Do I come anywhere close
when I say goodbye to vertebrae
sixth, eighth and twelfth thoracic
perhaps also linked with cosmic
structures that used to hold the city
of my body upright against the storms
of life?

Destruction still comes out of a clear blue sky
bombs that lay Damascus low
on and on with never a thought for the beauty lost
and those who left, weep
weep for a world in ruins, weep
for the gates for ever crumbled and
for the loss of roses.

And yet Maya dreams
dreams as her fingers strike the crystal notes
of the ancient Arabic qanun
Maya dreams of bombs metamorphosing
into white petals of peace.

But can the planets still hold the patterns of the seven
gates?
Let us dream in the magic of the night
let us dream the rebuilding
and one day

the Great Return.

9 July 2018

The Ides of March

the great emptiness
when touch is blind
and the word is constrained
to a screen and the polluted
airwaves

we need to relax down into
the bright sun of
springing nature
white violets on a bank
goldfinches on the teasel
the rough call of crows

you can find it all inside
where we meet in the heart fire
spirit kindled

sacred trust comes awake
in this hollowed out place where
hope dances with the midges
above the paving stones

let's meet beyond
infection, isolation
feel how love spreads
now
in the space made
by the emptiness of the known world

25 March 2020

Polly

The petals fall
as they must
for the fruit to set
delicate white signals
of the ripeness to come
and so you pass
gently into the light
leaving us your growing certainty
your joy
your presence
spreading around us in huge
clouds of hope

Lead us on
pollinate our hearts with
growing courage for
the Earth
ripening conviction of
Rebirth

For Polly Higgins, founder of Stop Ecocide, 22 April 2019

Spirit of Shades

Spirit of Shades
who conjures up these dim grey skies,
tightening your claws of cold
gripped tight into our tensed up backs;

even the blue cosmos shivers,
cross-hatched by lines of impossible clouds
out beyond these thick blank drapes,
where birds are our only streaks of hope,
seeking their feast of scarlet fruits
in twig tangled hedges, bush and tree
along these twisting Cotswold lanes.

We will hold midwinter at bay,
always awake, ever alert,
with hearts afire, blood aroused
in protest for the truth you hide
behind these vast grey cloaks of lies
and secret-woven shadows.

Truth is a flame we guard through the dark
a candle hidden deep and secure
from electric reach of those who serve
the sticky coils of control and fear.
Spirit of Shades we are not beguiled;
we see you at work behind the screens,
the towers and wires, the plugs and the switches
where souls are ensnared and extradited
to realms of steel and shards of ice.

But here where we sit and here where we stand,
holding the future in our hands,
in the heart of the dark the flame is awake.
Spirit of Shades you are not the master.
The fire of love is the king of the winter.

17 November 2019

8

Miscellaneous

A Poetry Reading

What if the tools, these
our five familiar senses,
are blunted from
constant use,
use through centuries
of accepted reality?

Maybe, knowing this, we'd
deploy other, stranger antennae.

We might see, right here,
we inhabit something
beyond location,
time having girth and height,
and space, duration.

What if, here, we standing at the bar, or
rolling words around like multicoloured marbles,
skipping, deftfoot, in and out of metaphors,
as the rope turns and turns and we gauge the moment
to enter the game;
what if here there's an underlay of pain?
What if here, there are layers of time,
multiples of meaning,
events kaleidoscoping in patterns:
innocent women burned alive as witches,
battles played out,
religious wars, treadmill, toil and blood?

What would we do if we knew,
if we felt it?
Would we dare to open

to the fields of time, the passage of place,
listening to each other
from a new heart space?

Communion

When we stand together with intent
we are a door
a gateway between trees
an alignment between stones
marking sunrise at solstice
marking star-rise in the velvet black
a single beam of focused possibilities
a capstone placed on a pyramid knowingly
and trusting what we know
timely
a message from Earth to Cosmos
and back multiplied
ancient archetypes re-embodying
harmonics of the lost chord resounding
frequency of unimaginable beginnings

We are coming closer to the mystery

We are a door
when we stand together

9 December 2010

Echo Chamber

Death is not one time only
Echo chamber of the aeons
Reverberating in the space around you
Invading your later years with challenges
You were never taught to read aright

Your body wades through a haunting
No doctor can diagnose
For which there are no familiar tools to unlock
The stories like rocks you must negotiate
Bare souled with stertorous breath

Our culture like a desert wind
Blows sterile dust in our faces
Where once the trees held our deaths
In sacred silence and we would walk
Among them listening
Letting them speak
Freeing the fear and the pain
From our overloaded bodies

Death was never one time only
You stand straighter with every passing
You release with blessing

1 September 2016

Hard Place

Not only you and I
but we and we all
Earth all over we all
are entering
the narrows, the neck of things, the hard place ...
tight, in, through, down, out.
It is bone cracking.
Agents, arms and agendas,
the chaos of the world,
cannot survive the singleness of this heart wringing simplicity.
We each and oh so only
go through alone and 'I' opening into where it is first time
like the silk fringed leaf
unfurling always into spring light.
This side we have choice,
we can be moment by moment here meeting in the clear beginning
    of each who we all are.
It is the opening ... into peace.

13 September and 17 October 2003

No Reference Points

Along with those, so many now,
whose letting go unravels their age
in a sudden burst of birth,
old memories are leaving,
rising from their comfortable armchairs,
no longer needing their structures,
books, potted plants,
their things,
moments fixed in black, white and sepia.
Old memories are passing through a curtain
of fine rain,
over a threshold
into light.
Even yesterday dissolves
beyond recall.

Who are you, am I, are we,
without them?
Shapeless, immaterial, unmortal,
a consciousness without reference points?

We are nothing special,
forerunners perhaps,
trailing songs like ribbons in the wind.

Thrown from our familiar mounts,
bruised, open, becoming incipient points of shine,
we meet a portal into an unborn world,
a glow, a warmth, no material boundaries,
we are one to one, one into one,
no separation …
heralds of the sun?

Heart to heart here
unbelievably
first time
we are one another.

23 June 2011

The Drop

We are all walking on the high line now over the long drop
balanced
eyes straight ahead
focused on the far side.
You'd lose it, if you dared look down.
A chasm waits below
secret and dark
shadows you have not owned
multiple, world wide.
Here is where fear lurks tentacled, hidden.
But can you sing, as you feel for each uncertain step
aiming for sunlight
and the green living earth,
with your heart in your mouth?
For you hold equilibrium at your centre
your safety harness, strong as love
stronger than every challenge.

Inspired by Chloe Levaillant, who walks barefoot on a
loose rope over deep chasms while singing, 7 April 2022

The Lay of Sir Lucifon

Sir Lucifon was a knight of the word,
A knight of the pen was he.
As you shall hear, his chosen quest
Turned out most wondrously.

Sir Lucifon set out to write
The lay beyond all lays,
And none but he should write that light,
Though it take him a thousand days.

He wrote it high, he wrote it low,
Long hand to furrowed brow.
His steed it was a mighty will
That never a fear would show.

Both rhyme and rule he held in scorn,
Of metre he would have none,
And none but the Heart should be his guide
But, alas, she was not at home.

Through brake and briar he spurred his steed,
Through many a dark of soul.
Oft-times he would rest on a fair maid's breast,
Still mindful of his goal.

And one she gave him a flow of words,
Another a dish of dreams,
But all he desired was the Lady Heart
And the secret that Lady sings.

One she gave him a crystal, another a thorn
And a third gave her fair body

And the dark of her eye and the white of her thigh.
'"Tis the Heart I desire,' said he.

One she gave him a spell, another a rune
And a mantra of secret power,
And the last gave him blood from the dark of the moon,
From a casket she kept in her bower.

And still he wrote over boulder and crag,
Through grim hollow and lonesome glen,
And nothing escaped his tireless eye
And no one escaped his pen.

Times he espied the elusive Heart,
The Rose of his deepest desire,
And he spurred him on to yet hardier feats
And he tempered his pen in the fire.

Sir Lucifon cried, 'I will have the Heart.
I will meet with her face to face.'
And he sharpened his pen both subtle and keen
And he rode to the meeting place.

With his silken words and his sharpened pen
Sir Lucifon tried the ground,
And deftly he sliced through breast and through bone,
And red grew the open wound.

Gently he reached in his hand and he clasped,
With tears of relief and joy,
The pulsing and beautiful Lady Heart.
'At last she is mine,' said he.

And away and away on his tireless steed
He rode with the Lady Heart,

And he sat him down to the lay of all lays
With courage renewed to start.

But e'er the morn with frosty eye
Had touched the edge of day
The Lady Heart had upped and gone
And silently hastened away.

And there in her place the familiar crack
That never a one could fill,
And Sir Lucifon lay at a loss for words,
And the work was unfinished still.

And as he lay and as he wept
For the lay he might never complete
There came to his window a humble bird
With his song and his breast of red.

'No one but you alone,' he sang.
'Nothing and no one.
You seek the Rose in the world,' he sang,
'But there she is not at home.'

Sir Lucifon laid down his pen
And opened the casement wide,
And somewhere within that hollow breast,
A bud stirred deep inside.

'I sought her high, I sought her low
To fill this lonely void.
The Rose of my dreams, the Lady Heart,
It was my own,' he said.

*Inspired by the Flemish tale of Sir Halewyn
(as retold by Alan Garner), 17 December 1990*

9

Spiritual

Our Mother

Our mother
You who are the
deep temple
of the living Earth

The song of Your sacred name
resounds
in the shimmering pathways
of our resurrecting bodies

Your realm of
nurturing warmth and abundance
is the womb
from which we awaken
into our true being

From the core of Your
glimmering darkness
Your ever constant intent is
the birth of love
flooding all creation
from within

We receive with gratitude each day
the selfless outpouring
of Your being

Your radiant presence
empowers our loving forgiveness
that we may honour and respect
our earthly vessels as the
shining temples they truly are

We commit ourselves
in reverence and love
to Your cycles of living and dying
unfolding and releasing

Within Your loving being
is born the power of the human I
to direct all that is astray
into its place of healing

For You
our Mother
are the soil of our growth and becoming
the portal and the power of our birthing
and within the ever renewing glory of Your love
shines
the circle
of our freedom

It is so

8 August 1997

Mary

My body's the boat that will bring you to shore
My life is the mast and my deed is the oar
My songs are the sails and my soul is the wind
And my words are the swift birds before and behind
All my being is nothing but vessel for thee
May the tale of thy coming be spoken through me

Madonna

After la Belle Verrière window at Chartres Cathedral

Born out of the living waters
and held here close to my breast,
this Child of the farthest universe
with me has come to rest.

Nourished by light invisible,
this Child, within my care,
shall grow in love and healing warmth
for all the world to share.

I am the Earth as Mother;
each one of us is she,
nurturing this pure and holy Child,
that the true I AM may be.

Magdalene

Trust is the ground she walked upon
trust in the fire that burned
in her sun centre
fire kindled before birth
trust in the guidance of that flame.
Those were no devils
the seven teachings learned
from her Body Fire
learned from the ancient sources of
the Mother Mysteries, a knowing rooted
in the Deep Light
of early humanity.
Trust it was that guided her to the
Incarnation of the Logos
and then
then at last
the Old Mother cults
could be released.
Her knowing body, her burning heart
opened to the New Ground,
kindling profound understanding:
Death was to become Life
straight down through
a penetration, a rekindling of the Deep Light
where woman is the Hierophant,
as she was then and still is,
and the Earth is becoming a Chalice
to the Sun.
Let trust be *our* ground.

20 September 2020

Easter Dawn

When under the rock the red rose lies
and the wake is folded way
Mary alone in the garden walks
in the early day

The stillness holds each drop of dew
suspended in its own light
there is nothing here yet to reflect
nothing alight

Under the fennel the soil is grey
empty as Mary's heart
the dust is dumb and speaks no trace
of what once the finger wrote

But the smallest breath stirs the fennel then
a soft hand shifts the gloom
where she stands alert by the rock, behold
the rose has gone

Her body becoming a tunèd ear
to the tiniest pulse is close
and, petal on crimson petal, the rose
unfolds from the abyss

Along every vein its sweet tide runs
her heart is no longer alone
Earth opens her hills like the cup of the moon
and she holds … the sun, the sun

The Garden

Near the Place of the Skull
we know there was a garden
and an empty tomb
as yet unused.
Someone must have tended
the garden,
planted fennel, rosemary, lavender
in preparation for a burial.

Because the tomb was nearby
they laid him there
the Crucified One
wrapped in white linen
with the customary spices
and they closed the tomb
with a stone.

In the dark of early morning
after the Sabbath
Mary came
weeping before the tomb
and the stone gone.
The angels asked her
Why do you weep?

Distraught
she replied
Because they have taken my Lord
and I do not know where they have laid Him.

Then turning, she saw Christ
standing there.

She thought He was the gardener.
And indeed He is
the gardener of souls
and we are the garden,
from that moment ...

awakening to the Sun within.

1 March 2015

Wild Man

He took the desert by storm
and he peopled it
with the words he forbore to use
he let them slip away from him
so easily
like a woman who is used to giving birth
he let them blow away
till he was empty
as hollow as the tall dark jars
the women folk carry
fetching cool water
to fetch the well water home
and he wore the desert outside in
wearing its jaggedness next to his skin
that wild he was

Before Anthony and Paul
he faced them
the siren, the wraith and mirage
and they used his own words
to embody themselves
and they came back to taunt and to jeer
and they grappled him down
till his breath was a gasp
and they left him for dead on the hot red stones
stretched out wordlessly
under the desert stars
under the great desert moon
but he rose and took his own death on his back
gently for fear it might tumble or crack
that wild he was

And the desert turned around then
and looked at him
and she opened her secret door
his scant needs were met
abundantly
and the sun built a nest in his heart
and his words were returned to him
so resonant
the wind was amazed and took flight
in his bones they were humming
in his blood they were thrumming
guiding his feet toward home
and he walked till he came to Jordan's shore
round about and hidden was his pathway there
that wild he was

And he said I will baptise you with water
the waters of the womb he said
but one will come after
baptising with spirit
one will come after
baptising with spirit
one will come after baptising with spirit
my words are vessels
waiting for filling
vessels
but He is the wine

After the Funeral

For Simon

How is it we are not aware
when blessings come,
'dropping like the gentle rain
from heaven', when
even the spring flowers know it,
in gratitude for visits
from infrequent bees
and angels dip into our sleep
bringing unexpected peace?

You baked our daily bread for us
in continual service,
quietly giving,
and your smiles
warmed community
wherever you walked.

Maybe, at your passage into
beyond our knowing,
we could wake to what
moves among us, even in times
of grief and darkness,

giving us courage
to go on.

9 March 2024

10

Rose

Rejuvenation

When the rain comes down
I forgive the cracks and creases
on this earth skin I have been wearing
for decades

Does the Earth forgive our
lack of love she has worn
for centuries?

Now, with the cool downpour
racing along roadside gutters,
soaking the pale and dried out
garden lawns,
the grass can breathe and
my heart lets out a green cloud
of hope,
suffusing limbs, torso
and tired joints

I undo my sandals …
my feet smile at the blissful moisture

When the rain comes I remember
how it was to be young

For a moment the Earth
is my home again

18 July 2025

Birthday Poem for Rob

Have you observed
with what intensity
the bee negotiates the
labyrinth of the full flowering
rose ...
all for the pollen?

Such intent lies in
every spoonful of sweetness
the bees gift us
under the summer sun.

Seeking meaning, we do not always
aim unerringly,
we get diverted by the twists of fortune,
the turns of pain,
forgetting it is always
a labyrinth,
the way to the centre,
and we lose focused will.

Watch the bees,
follow the perfume,
savour the honey.

16 May 2025

Truth

There are rules concerning
what may be uncovered.
Revelation, emblazoned on the heart,
calls down punishment
over centuries; even now we may not
utter names, but
they emerge
despite ourselves
and the threat of prison.

You cannot stop the opening
of petals, unforced but utterly determined,
unfolding stage by stage, golden,
when her time has come,

the unstoppable
secret centre
of the rose.

7 October 2024

Also available from Awen Publications:

Tidal Shift: selected poems
Mary Palmer

Knowing her end was near, Mary Palmer worked on her poems, compiling her very best and writing new ones with a feverish intensity. This is the result, published here with her full cooperation and consent. These are poems from the extreme edge and very centre of life – words of light that defy death's shadow with a startling intensity, clarity, and honesty. Containing poems from across Mary's career, selected by Jay Ramsay, *Tidal Shift* is an impressive legacy from a poet of soul and insight.

Poetry ISBN 978-1-906900-09-0 £9.99

Crackle of Almonds: selected poems
Gabriel Bradford Millar

In these renegade poems ranging from 1958 to 2011 Gabriel Bradford Millar presents a spectrum of life, in all its piquant poignancy, with unfaltering precision, defiance, and finesse. From the very first to the very last, the breathtaking skill of this consummate wordsmith does not waver. Many of the poems linger in the air – not least because Millar performs them orally with such verve. These epicurean poems not only offer a lasting testimony to a life well-lived, but inspire the reader to live well too

Poetry ISBN 978-1-906900-29-8 £9.99

Pilgrimage: a journey to Love Island
Jay Ramsay

In the summer of 1990 Jay Ramsay set out on pilgrimage with an interfaith group from London to Iona. The result is his most ambitious book-length poem. Epiphanic, conversational, meditational, psychological, political, it divines 'the cross' of spiritual and ecological being in Britain's radical tradition, as symbolised by Iona as the crown of the Celtic church and the direction that Christianity lost. Full of stories, reflections, memories, and images, *Pilgrimage* is above all a love poem, an invitation into the greater love that is our true becoming where we can find the God most personal to all of us – alive in the heart of Life.

Poetry/Spirituality ISBN 978-1906900-54-0 £15.00

www.ingramcontent.com/pod-product-compliance
Lightning Source LLC
LaVergne TN
LVHW011336080426
835513LV00006B/386